Niggas & Flies

To all Black people
tired of hearing, "Us niggas,"
and ready to start interjecting,
"You mean, you niggas."

Niggas & Flies

Written By
Mylia Tiye Mal Jaza

Cover Design By
Sun Child Wind Spirit

Proofread By
Goddess Sage

Edited By
Dr. Mari Michelle

Niggas & Flies

First Edition. Printed In the USA.
Recycled Paper Encouraged.

ISBN-10: 1540310981
ISBN-13: 978-1-5403-1098-9

Author
Mylia Tiye Mal Jaza
GoddessSage@bepublished.biz
www.myliajaza.gqnu.net

Self-Publishing Associate
Mary M. Jefferson
BePublished.Org - Chicago
(972) 880-8316
www.bepublished.org
www.maryjefferson.us
mari@bepublished.org

Imprint of Record
CreateSpace On-Demand Publishing
7290-B Investment Drive
Charleston, SC 29418

Table of Content

Chapter 1
The Looming Lures

People love playing games. They sometimes don't know when it's time to quit. Often, they won't even fathom the idea of stopping if the game they're playing involves either your loss or demise. This is especially true when people are playing word games, and the words they are using directly affect you with detrimental effects throughout your lifetime.

Take the words "nigger" and "nigga" as examples of this type of dangerous word game. These two words have been a part of the English vernacular for hundreds of years. Americans pronouncing the base word properly enunciate the "er," while those using slang or broken English prefer enunciating the "a." Despite the spelling or pronunciation, the derogatory nature remains the same – a word describing a shiftless, good-for-nothing thief.

However, since so many racist people of European descent commonly used these degrading words to refer to people of African ancestry, many Nubian Americans became so used to being called "nigger" and "nigga" by the 1960s that they began referring to themselves and other Blacks as niggas. In the 1970s, referring to each other as Black Kings and Queens began and started noticeably taking root in the 80s. By the 1990s, nigga became popularized as gangsta rappers bragged about gunning down niggas and hip-hop artists boasted about being a proud nigga.

When the new millennium hit, some of the same people loving nigga and saying it was now a term of endearment, including street hustlers and underbellies of society, began taking issue with Whites casually saying nigga around Blacks. Around this same time, many Blacks who never lost their regal focus began fighting against nigga by adding God and Goddess to the discourse. Still, nigga went mainstream and threatened to silence positive perceptions of Black Americans in and outside our communities.

Now, in 2017, it seems the issue of "The N-Word" has blown up in the face of America, as it has in the past, but this time it is a little different.

I am thankful for movements such as Black Lives Matter that address police brutality and the murder of unarmed Black men by cops. I wish there were organizations that also focused solely on the "Perception of Blackness" and "Preserving the Black Culture." I believe the first step toward any true protection of Black lives from overzealous police and unscrupulous thugs will require addressing the causes of such plights. The root of them all are in the perception of us Blacks.

I'll put it like this: The people in the nursing homes who don't get visitors are the ones most likely to be mistreated. Those whose relatives and friends drop in from time to time, that's who staffers assure they do right by even if they don't feel like going into the room. It's not right, but it's true. People who do not care about you will treat you worse than others they don't care about when they see that you don't have anybody around who cares about or loves you.

When people see that your own looks down on you, how can they be expected to hold you in any high regard? Even the best person in the world would think twice about you if they find out those closest to you consider you as untrustworthy and good for nothing. Well, that's what being considered as a nigga insinuates. That's why I am baffled at why this word continues to be allowed by a community of people plagued with maltreatment partially because of it. I say partially because personal choice plays a role in everything any person does, despite whatever catalyst is in effect.

As Black people are increasingly targeted for murder by community criminals and police officers, the "term of endearment" role nigga plays can no longer be a mask for the "object of scorn" nigger is. Just like we fight off flies at our family reunions and other outings, we must be vigilant to rid New America of nigger by not allowing nigga either. When it is used, it should be accepted for what it is – just another cuss word like bitch or whore, and just another racial slur like honky, chink or wetback.

Chapter 2
Three Major Pests

There seems to be several things at play that keeps this word (perception) alive today, and each of these things vex my spirit and endanger the lives of Black people throughout America. To keep this simple, I'll just address my top three concerns and present it in a way that helps you understand how nigga (nigger) is really a small problem with an easy fix. It's just because it has been allowed to fester and get out of hand that it seems like us Black folks are forever doomed to have it flying around our heads.

To hear "nigger" is like seeing a dragonfly, you don't have to be close to it to cringe. Dragonflies are long with big wings. Some people call them snake doctors. Everybody immediately avoid contact with dragonflies. If you see one heading in your direction, you roll up your window if you're in a vehicle or you swat it away or move around if you are sitting outside. Nigger makes people act like that too.

To hear "nigga" is like seeing a housefly, you don't like it but you may not say or do anything about it. This common fly is also called a black fly. Sometimes we assume the little insect would fly back out the same door or window it flew in through. If we have food out or if we're outside, we gently fan it away and cover our food/drink to keep it from landing on/in it. The only time most people seem truly bothered by this particular fly is when it keeps buzzing around their ear after they get frustrated from swatting at it (as if it is intentionally targeting that person). Nigga has that same effect.

Then we have the "s" added, and that is the great equalizer. Experiencing niggers or niggas is like being locked in a room with a horsefly. Horseflies are big, have a loud buzz, and will bite you like it's stabbing you. In other words, you know you have a fight on your hands. And you know that, in this fight, either you will be harmed or you must prepare to kill. That's how all these niggas and niggers make me think.

I feel like I am under attack by people using words and by people living out the negative meanings of those words. I feel like I have to buck against these words and actions, just like I would protect and defend myself against anything endangering my health or life. I hate flies and know of the diseases they carry.

I also hate all forms, usages and displays of the N-Word and know all the dis-ease they cause. I would try to kill a housefly and dragonfly just as quick as I would try to kill a horsefly. The same with the words nigger, nigga and niggs. I will try to rid New America (Black America) of them all with one mighty blow. If that won't work, I'll whip out a travel-sized bottle of flying insect killer! Nigger and nigga must be extinguished.

Chapter 3
Three Relentless Scavengers

Yes, the main reasons why I want nigga to become obsolete are totally selfish. I want to see fewer Black youth considering themselves as savages. I want to see more Black men cease crime sprees and become business owners and providers for their children. I want to see more Black women value being a positive example over being the preferred lay.

I want to walk down the street and know that no Black man will try to harm me. I want to be anywhere and know that every Black person around can trust that I have their backs and I can trust that they have mine should some racist(s) suddenly go haywire. I want to not have to worry about whether my relatives will be shot by people who looks like us that just want to earn points to join a criminal group. I could go on and on, but you get my point.

I want it to be safe to be Black in America. This cannot happen if Black people act like our only threats are police. We have three terrible elements feasting off our communities and posing far greater threats than the police. It's because of these relentless scavengers that cops usually end up coming to our homes and communities in the first place.

People being upheld in their wrongdoing by their relatives are a huge problem in the Black community. We see it every time someone is robbed or a house is burglarized, and suddenly everyone in the neighborhood is quiet except the family harmed. Those who do speak up usually only say, "I ain't no snitch-ass nigga. I don't know nothing." But when a reward is offered or their household is the next one rocked by a thieving relative, they say, "Turn dat nigga in."

This is the equivalent of fruit flies allowed to live among the apple trees and berry bushes. If the nature of the pest is to eat your good fruit and that which you discard (bad fruit) and you allow it to multiply, how can you expect to continually sustain its appetite and think its greed and mania won't overtake your (its) dwelling place at some point?

A second group of scavengers flying around the Black community are flesh flies. These are the people who get custody of kids for the checks, but they abuse the children. Some are adoptive parents, some are foster parents, others are fake god-parents, and most are biological parents who are more concerned with living their own life than grooming youths to better navigate theirs.

Happy, sad, living or dead, human life really doesn't matter to people who identify as niggas but have a flesh fly nature. The only life that matters is their own lives in the limelight or good life at any price. They will pimp the children in their care, set you up as a mark for kidnapping and organ snatching, and will unload a semi-automatic weapon at your 3-year-old's birthday party with no remorse.

The blowfly is the most prevalent type of non-violent scavenger mentality I've seen flying around some Black people. These are the people who do not think they can identify as niggas unless they are constantly involved in, starting and surrounded by, negativity. They make it a point to start trouble everywhere they go, be rude to everyone they meet, and act like a spoiled little girl starving for attention when they show up anywhere.

You can be having a good time at a black-tie gala or be feeling on top of the world at a barbecue, and a death-and-feces loving shiny thing will show up, show out, and shut the party down by being an intentional ass. People hating to see others happy or successful is not new, neither is people sabotaging moments of celebration for others. These types of people also shoot your dreams and aspirations down the moment you verbalize them.

But, blowflies are also not unique to the Black community. Every community of people seems to be used to these problems, so much so that when planning festive events with friends and family they all have to intentionally skip inviting certain people (yet expect them to disrespect expressed wishes and show up anyway). They may look prettier than the other flies pestering people, but they pose the same threat to our health.

It doesn't matter the kind of fly, it's not safe to let linger. Neither does applying "a" instead of "er" to "nigg" make it okay to use. Truth is universal. Since nigger is wrong for White people to call people, it is wrong for Black people to call people. And, if nigga is okay for Black people to call themselves, it is okay for White people to call themselves that too. Otherwise, if nigga is bad for non-Blacks to say period, it is bad for Blacks to say too. Kill these flies!

Chapter 4
A Race Misidentified

Nigga is not synonymous with Negro. Negro does not mean "man without a head." Negro is the Spanish word for Black. I identify with the words Negro and Black. A lot of people of African descent don't like being called Black and say things like, "I'm brown" or "I'm light-skinned." That's why many refer to our race as African Americans. I consider people born in Africa who eventually became American citizens as African Americans.

Because of this "identity crisis," our internal struggle has become heightened. We now have pervasive ignorance dominating our dialogue, idolatry throughout our churches, and are readily seen praising people for simply stacking money instead of supporting those who are standing on principles. We have fallen very low as a race, and refuse to take a selfie with the flash on to remove ourselves from the sunken place.

The "nigga" misnomer is keeping the Black community locked into niggerdom by facilitating niggardly behavior and promoting niggatry to the broken males and desperate females parents with a nigger mentality created and turned loose early. Because the images of hoodrats and street thugs keep being perpetuated as the top elements of Black society, educated and hardworking Blacks are treated like (and called) niggers and niggas on a daily basis by people of all races.

For any person to posture self as speaking for an entire race is an effort already out of balance. I know there are a number of Black people who call themselves niggas. There are now people of every race who refer to themselves as niggas. Those people are not my concern. They know exactly what they are, and I am not in a position to tell anyone they are something other than what they consider themselves to be. All I want to be sure to make crystal clear is the fact that I am Black and not a nigger/nigga under any circumstance.

Don't get me wrong. I know every human alive is prone to nigger behavior and a nigga mentality. I'm not immune to making bad choices and displaying terrible behavior either. But just like I can correct my thoughts and behavior, anybody else can too. And, just because I choose to live a life doing any and every foul thing under the sun, that doesn't mean I should define or categorize you the same way I do myself.

If you love doing nigger shit and take pride in calling yourself a nigga, do that but leave Black people out of it. We Negroes have enough problems of our own, and are constantly having to remind ourselves that what other groups are trying to say is our shit too is so not our shit but their own. Asian plight is the Asian's to own and repair. The same is true for Blacks, Whites, gays, immigrants, and niggas.

The time has come for the Black community to stop allowing itself to be burdened by the terrors of niggers and the label of nigga. Only by Black Americans standing up and openly shunning use of "The N-Word" in all its forms by all its speakers can Negro Americans truly begin to expect better treatment from fellow Blacks and ultimately people outside the race.

Honestly, until Blacks identify ourselves by a single name, we should passionately fight against passively allowing those who benefit from degrading Black culture to define us as niggers and tell the world Negroes accept the label nigga and want a monopoly on it. And, since every race deserves acknowledgement, I recommend that in addition to adding "Mixed" as an option to applications asking for race to be disclosed, a category of "Nigga" can be added to so even that undeniable race isn't lumped unfairly with Blacks and other groups.

After all, nigger is a lifestyle and niggas do have their own language, music and culture. A nigga probably hate being called Black just as much as my proud Black ass hate being called nigger or nigga. Them pulling themselves away from identifying as members of the Negro race will help Blacks/African Americans and niggas focus on enriching and protecting their communities with less confusion and more distinction.

THE ART & ARTIST

Published with the assistance of BePublished.Org, **Niggas & Flies** is Mylia Tiye Mal Jaza's 21st published book. It is the author's first work solely devoted to addressing "The N-Word" debate and its need for rejection by the Black community at-large.

"With so many attacks directed at Blacks today, allowing ourselves to be further victimized by not addressing the way we're generally perceived is suicide," Jaza contends. "Although I couldn't go into the detail I wanted because I didn't want to risk confusing readers with side issues, I hope the main message resounds. Blacks are not niggers and niggas isn't an acceptable label for us either, no matter what rap artist says otherwise."

Niggas & Flies is available for order worldwide from bricks-and-mortar and online book retailers including Barnes & Noble, your local bookstore, and Amazon.Com.

THE AUTHOR

Mylia Tiye Mal Jaza (Mary "Mari" Michelle Jefferson) is a former Texas resident and Mississippi native presently residing in Illinois. She graduated from Jackson State University and the University of Texas at Dallas, and holds an honorary doctorate degree from Trinity Evangelical Christian University.

The entrepreneur, former professional model, and wedding officiant is also an award-winning journalist who gives back to the communities in which she lives and conducts business by mentoring teens, cleaning highways, feeding the homeless, providing gifts to nursing home residents, organizing community art exhibits and music festivals, and conducting school supplies drives for youth.

Also known as Sun Child Wind Spirit, Jaza (aka Goddess Sage) is a vocalist who has performed alongside international artists and at popular venues. She also helps writers with an array of editorial and business services including self-publishing and promotions training through BePublished.Org.

Prior to the June 2017 release of **Niggas & Flies**, three of Mylia's published books were works she published that were written by ancestors and relatives of hers – The Facts Of Reconstruction *by John R. Lynch*, The Old

Negro And The New Negro *by T. Leroy Jefferson, M.D.*, and Mother's Mantras *by Susie W. Jefferson*.

Mylia's other books were original works she created that ranged in content from poetry and prose to film and television scripts. The titles include: Life Is Beautiful: La Vita E Bella, Life Is Beautiful: La Vita Es Hermosa, Seen In Other Words, Plea For Peace, All For Show, Scientific Evidence God Exists, Elegies Of A Goddess, AND, Get Off Your Packages, My Plan For Every Bully, Stop & Tie Your Shoes, P.E.N.I.S., FOOLISH OF ME: Addressing Love Unappreciated, Amour Noir and Sweet Mary.

MarryUsNow.us   MaryJefferson.us   BePublished.org

Order Books By Mylia Jaza & Family

Life Is Beautiful:
La Vita E Bella
$20/soft x _____

The Old Negro And The New Negro
by T. Leroy Jefferson M.D.
_____ x $20/soft
_____ x $35/hard

Life Is Beautiful:
La Vita Es Hermosa
$15/soft x _____

All For Show:
Film & Television Scripts
_____ x $25/soft

Seen In Other Words
$10/soft x _____

Plea For Peace
_____ x $10/soft

The Facts Of Reconstruction
by John R. Lynch
$25/soft x _____

Scientific Evidence
God Exists
_____ x $15/soft
_____ x $30/hard

AND
$15/soft x _____

Elegies Of A Goddess
_____ x $15/soft

READER _____

ADDRESS _____ UNIT # _____

CITY _____ ST _____ ZIP _____

EMAIL _____ COUNTY _____ COUNTRY _____

Remit Payment For Selected Books + Form + $5 s/h To:

Mary M. Jefferson
P.O. Box 8324
Jackson, MS 39284

*Please allow three (3) weeks minimum delivery to
allow for order processing, autographing of books, and shipment
to your address provided above.*

Which Book(s) Autographed Using Which Individual(s) Name(s):

_____

_____

_____

_____

Your Thoughts About Recipient(s):

_____

_____

_____

_____

Personal Message From You To Author(s):

_____

_____

_____

_____

_____

_____

_____

Children's Book
The Animals *by Isaiah Walls Palmer*
$25/soft x _____

Cat's Colors *by Kelvin T. Johnson*
Children's Book
_____ x $25/soft

The Artistic Sketch Of Me
by Latisha A. Jefferson
$20/soft x _____

My Plan For Every Bully
Children's Book
_____ x $25/soft

Stop And Tie Your Shoes
$20/soft x _____

Get Off Your Packages
_____ x $20/soft

P.E.N.I.S.
$20/soft x _____

When The Quarterback Got Cut
_____ x $20/soft

Mother's Mantras
by Susie W. Jefferson
$20/soft x _____

Foolish of Me:
Addressing Love Unappreciated
_____ x $20/soft

READER _____

ADDRESS _____ UNIT # _____

CITY _____ ST _____ ZIP _____

EMAIL _____ COUNTY _____ COUNTRY _____

Remit Payment For Selected Books + Form + $5 s/h To:
Mary M. Jefferson
P.O. Box 8324
Jackson, MS 39284

Please allow three (3) weeks minimum delivery to allow for order processing, autographing of books, and shipment to your address provided to us above.

Which Book(s) Autographed Using Which Individual(s) Name(s):

_____

_____

_____

_____

Your Thoughts About Recipient(s):

_____

_____

_____

_____

Personal Message From You To Author(s):

_____

_____

_____

_____

_____

_____

_____

_____

Other Books By Mylia Jaza & Family

Thank you for your support.

 Amour Noir
$20/soft x _____

From My Facebook Friends
_____ x $15/soft

 Sweet Mary:
Infused Food & Beverage Offering
$25/soft x _____

Niggas & Flies
_____ x $15/soft

READER _____

ADDRESS _____ UNIT # _____

CITY _____ ST _____ ZIP _____

EMAIL _____ COUNTY _____ COUNTRY _____

Remit Payment For Selected Books + Form + $5 s/h To:
Mary M. Jefferson
P.O. Box 8324
Jackson, MS 39284

*Please allow three (3) weeks minimum delivery to allow for order processing,
autographing of books, and shipment to your address provided to us above.*

Which Book(s) Autographed Using Which Individual(s) Name(s):

_____

_____

_____

_____

Your Thoughts About Recipient(s):

_____

_____

_____

_____

Personal Message From You To Author(s):

_____

_____

_____

_____

_____

_____

_____